FUNDAMENTALS
OF THE
FAITH

13 LESSONS TO GROW IN THE GRACE
& KNOWLEDGE OF JESUS CHRIST

INTRODUCTION BY

JOHN MACARTHUR

MOODY PUBLISHERS
CHICAGO

Earlier editions published by Grace Community Church. Editor of 2009 edition: Dave Amandus

Cover Design: Dog Eared Design
Cover Image: iStock and Getty images

ISBN: 978-0-8024-3839-3

We hope you enjoy this book from Moody Publishers. Our goal is to provide high-quality, thought-provoking books and products that connect truth to your real needs and challenges. For more information on other books and products written and produced from a biblical perspective, go to www.moodypublishers.com or write to:

Moody Publishers
820 N. LaSalle Boulevard
Chicago, IL 60610

This book is printed on acid free recycled paper containing 30% PCW (Post Consumer Waste) and manufactured in the United States of America by Versa Press.

5 7 9 10 8 6

Printed in the United States of America

Produced with the assistance of The Livingstone Corporation (www.livingstonecorp.com). Project staff includes Neil Wilson and Linda Taylor. Interior design by Larry Taylor. Typeset by Troy Ristow, Tom Ristow, and Kathy Ristow.

WELCOME AND INTRODUCTION

Fundamentals of the Faith (*FOF*) may be the best-kept secret at Grace Community Church.

It was born out of a joyful necessity decades ago when I was a young pastor and Grace Church was relatively small. We were growing. Families and individuals—some new to the faith and others simply new to the area—were coming to the church in droves. So many new faces. So many unique backgrounds. We needed to ensure this growing congregation was firmly rooted in the fundamental doctrines of the faith.

FOF has played a key role in the spiritual growth of our congregation ever since. It provides new believers with a rock solid theological foundation. It helps more mature Christians sharpen their understanding of key doctrines and equips them for evangelism and discipleship. It fosters the only kind of unity that truly means anything in the church—unity based on a shared understanding of God's truth.

In spite of its importance to Grace Church through the years, *FOF* remains, as I have said, somewhat of a secret. Except for a handful of churches, its resources have been largely untapped.

That is, until now. By God's grace, we now have a platform from which we can put this powerful resource into churches across the country. What you hold in your hands has undergone decades of refining. It is the fruit of many years of preparation, instruction, and application. Having been taught and tested in the classroom, it has proven itself effective through the lives it has influenced.

Of course, the power behind this curriculum is not in its format or layout, but in the Word of God on which it is based. We know that when the Holy Spirit uses His Word in peoples' hearts, their lives are transformed. And that's why I am so thrilled that these materials have found their way to you. *FOF* has welcomed thousands upon thousands of people into the church and into the family of Christ. It has helped believers build a spiritual foundation of solid rock.

I trust it will benefit you and your church in the same way.

[signature]

Pastor-Teacher

Grace Community Church

Sun Valley, California

CONTENTS

INTRODUCTION

The *Fundamentals of the Faith* (*FOF*) Bible study has become foundational to the life of Grace Community Church. It is used for our new believers' classes, for evangelistic outreaches, and as an introduction to what our church believes. A typical class has about 10 students. Some are non-Christians taking the class because a friend encouraged them to. Others are seasoned saints looking to be refreshed on the basic doctrines of our faith. This diverse environment encourages interaction between teacher and students, and this interaction often forms relationships that last a lifetime. The size of the classes allows them to function effectively as small groups and minimize the tendency for the teacher to "lecture" or "sermonize" the material. Class members who complete the assigned lessons and participate in the discussions report great benefits from this study.

A common testimony at Grace Community Church is from people who thought they were saved and then took an *FOF* class, only to see that they did not really understand the gospel. Through the class they finally learned the truth about Christianity and then saw their lives transformed by the gospel. It is impossible to tell how many people have come to saving faith through these classes, but it is easily the most effective evangelistic tool we have used.

FOF is the outgrowth of the belief that the essence of Christianity is truth—truth about God the Father, Christ, and the Holy Spirit; truth about man's sin and God's plan of salvation; and truth about God's revealed will for the church and our individual lives. What you believe matters, and it matters eternally. Wrong beliefs about God lead people to hell (Matthew 7:22–23). Christianity is a faith anchored on the truths in the Bible, which is God's only inspired written revelation.

This material is best used in a small group of committed people. If you commit to attending these classes, doing the work beforehand, and participating, you will gain an increased understanding of the fundamentals of the Christian faith.

HOW TO USE THE LESSON ASSIGNMENTS

Fundamentals of the Faith (*FOF*) Class Basics:

1. Prepare for each session by downloading the assignment message from www.gty.org/fof, taking notes and identifying questions you may have, and filling in the answers in the workbook. You will need your Bible handy while you complete the assignments and when you are in the class sessions.

2. The class or group sessions will *not* involve filling in the answers in the workbook. Class time will be used to expand and discuss key topics within the lesson and to answer any questions that you have relative to the lesson.

3. The better you prepare, the better you will be able to participate and the more you will benefit from the class interaction.

4. Come prepared to interact and learn.

INTRODUCTION TO THE BIBLE

Prepare for Your Assignment

1. Along with this workbook, you will need a Bible and a journal or notebook for personal notes from the message you will hear.

2. Download message #1, "Our God-Breathed Bible," from www.gty.org/fof.

3. Using your Bible, fill in the answers on the following pages.

Memorize 2 Timothy 3:16

All Scripture is inspired by God and profitable for teaching, for reproof, for correction, for training in righteousness.

■ I hope you have an appreciation for the Scripture. I hope you have an appreciation for it not as a fetish but because it is the greatest treasure, apart from God Himself, that we have. It is His very word, His very self-revelation. When people ask me why it is that I systematically teach through book after book, why it is that I pay so much attention to detail and to every verse and every phrase and touch all the words, I tell them it's because I understand them to be the words of God revealed to us from Him. And I would not second-guess the necessity of those words being then presented, taught and understood by all of us.

John MacArthur

The Bible is the Word of God. It claims to be the truth, the message from God to man. Second Peter 1:21 says that "men moved by the Holy Spirit spoke from God."

- ♦ The Scriptures were written by approximately 40 different men.

- ♦ These men lived in several different countries and cultures.

- ♦ They lived in different eras (1400 B.C. through A.D. 90).

- ♦ They wrote in three languages: Hebrew, Aramaic, and Greek.

Despite these differences, God moved the writers to focus on His glory in man's redemption through one central figure— Jesus Christ, the Son of God.

I. The Old Testament (39 books)

A. The Pentateuch (5 books)

The first five books of the Old Testament were written by Moses around 1400 B.C. They often are referred to as the "Five Books of Moses" or the "Pentateuch."

List the books of the Pentateuch in the order you find them in your Bible.

1. _____ The book of beginnings: Creation, man, sin, redemption, God's nation

2. _____ God delivers His people from Egypt

3. _____ Atonement, holiness, and worship through sacrifice and purification

4. _____ God's people continually disobey and wander in the wilderness for 40 years

5. _____ Moses' great discourses to prepare Israel to enter the Promised Land

B. History (12 books)

The historical books were written between 1400 and 450 B.C. and describe God's dealings with His chosen people, Israel, the Hebrew nation.

List these books in the order you find them in your Bible.

1. _____ 5. _____ 9. _____

2. _____ 6. _____ 10. _____

3. _____ 7. _____ 11. _____

4. _____ 8. _____ 12. _____

C. Poetry (5 books)

The following five books are poetic, describing in poetry and song God's greatness and His dealings with men.

List these books in the order you find them in your Bible.

1. _____ The suffering and loyal trust of a man who loved God

2. _____ Songs of praise and instruction

3. _____ God's practical wisdom for daily life

4. _____ The emptiness of an earthly life without God

5. _____ A celebration of marital joy

D. Major Prophets (5 books)

A prophet was a person commissioned by God to deliver His message to men. These books are called "Major Prophets" because they generally are longer than the writings of the "Minor Prophets." The Major Prophets were written approximately between 750 and 550 B.C.

List these books in the order you find them in your Bible.

1. _____ 3. _____ 5. _____

2. _____ 4. _____

E. Minor Prophets (12 books)

The last 12 books of the Old Testament were written approximately between 840 and 400 B.C.

List these books in the order you find them in your Bible.

1. _____ 5. _____ 9. _____

2. _____ 6. _____ 10. _____

3. _____ 7. _____ 11. _____

4. _____ 8. _____ 12. _____

II. The New Testament (27 books)

The New Testament, or New Covenant, reveals Jesus Christ, the Redeemer of men. In it we find:

♦ The life of Christ

♦ The way of salvation

♦ The beginning of Christianity

♦ Instruction for Christian living

♦ God's plan for the future

A. History (5 books)
1. The Gospels (first 4 books)

a. _____ The life of Christ, written especially for the Jews, revealing Jesus Christ as their long-awaited Messiah

b. _____ The life of Christ, revealing Jesus as the obedient Servant of God; written especially to the Roman world

c. _____ The life of Christ, revealing Jesus as the perfect man, emphasizing His humanity; written by Luke, a Greek, to the Greek world

d. _____ The life of Christ, revealing Jesus as the Son of God, stressing His deity; very evangelistic

What two reasons are given for the writing of John's Gospel (John 20:31)?

1. _____

_____

2. _____

_____

_____

2. History of the Early Church (1 book)

_____ The beginning and spread of the Christian church; it could be called the "Acts of the Holy Spirit," and was written as an evangelistic tool

B. Letters or Epistles (21 books)
These books were written to individuals, to churches, or to believers in general. The letters deal with every aspect of Christian faith and responsibility.

List these books in the order you find them in your Bible.

1. Paul's Letters (13 books)

a. _____   h. _____

b. _____   i. _____

c. _____   j. _____

d. _____   k. _____

e. _____   l. _____

f. _____   m. _____

g. _____

2. General Letters (8 books)

a. _____   e. _____

b. _____   f. _____

c. _____   g. _____

d. _____   h. _____

C. Prophecy (1 book)
The last book of the New Testament tells of future events.

♦ Return of Christ

♦ Reign of Jesus Christ

♦ Glory of Jesus Christ

♦ Future state of believers and unbelievers

This book is called _____.

III. Christ in the Bible

A. The Old and New Testaments should be seen together, as both portray Jesus Christ as the central figure.
Read the following verses and fill in the blanks.

1. Luke 24:27. Christ is seen in _____.

2. John 5:39. Jesus said the Scriptures "bear witness of _____."

B. The key is Jesus.

5 Law	12 History	5 Poetry	17 Prophecy	4 Gospels	1 History	21 Letters	1 Prophecy
Promises of Christ	*Anticipation of Christ: Types, Experiences, and Prophecies*			*Manifestation of Christ*	*The Church of Christ*		*Coronation of Christ*

IV. Why Is the Bible Important?

When tempted by Satan, Jesus alluded to Deuteronomy 8:3: "Man shall not live on bread alone, but on every word that proceeds out of the mouth of God" (Matthew 4:4).

A. What does 2 Timothy 3:16 say about the Bible? (Choose the correct answer.)

☐ Some of the Bible is inspired by God.

☐ There are a few parts that are not inspired.

☐ The entire Bible is inspired by God.

☐ Only those parts that speak to us in a personal way are inspired by God.

■ The Old Testament is the revelation of God to show man what God is like, who God is, what God tolerates and does not tolerate, and how God desires holiness and punishes sin. The New Testament is God revealed by His Son in the life of His Son, in the message of His Son, in the understanding of the work of His Son, and in the culmination and the coming of His Son to establish His eternal kingdom. But in either case, Old Testament, New Testament, God spoke. And what we have is indeed the word of God. This is not the word of man.

So, men were not inspired but Scripture is. God breathed into them and they wrote it down, word by word what God breathed into them. It was more than dictation. They weren't just listening to some voice and writing mechanically every word; it was flowing through their heart and their soul and their mind and their emotions and their experiences. But it came out every word the Word of God. As God breathed into them the message and they were carried along by the Holy Spirit, they said it and some of them wrote it down. Miraculous, supernatural, inexplicable process that yields to us the Word of God.

John MacArthur

B. How do the following verses show the importance of God's Word?

1. 2 Timothy 3:15 _____

_____

_____

2. Hebrews 4:12 _____

_____

_____

C. What four things does God's Word do?

1. Psalm 19:7a _____

2. Psalm 19:7b _____

3. Psalm 19:8a _____

4. Psalm 19:8b _____

V. Application

Based on what you have learned about the Bible, what should your response be?

_____

_____

_____

_____

■ When it comes to godly living and godly service, to growing in "the discipline and instruction of the Lord" (Eph. 6:4), God-breathed Scripture provides for us the comprehensive and complete body of divine truth necessary to live as our heavenly Father desires for us to live. The wisdom and guidance for fulfilling everything He commands us to believe, think, say and do is found in His inerrant, authoritative, comprehensive, and complete Word.

It goes without saying that it is impossible to believe, understand, and follow what you do not even know. It is completely futile, as well as foolish, to expect to live a spiritual life without knowing spiritual truth. Biblically untaught believers, especially those in biblically untaught churches, are easy prey for false teachers. They are spiritual "children, tossed here and there by waves, and carried about by every wind of doctrine, by the trickery of men, by craftiness in deceitful scheming" (Eph. 4:14). Throughout most of redemptive history, God could have said what He said in Hosea's day: "My people are destroyed for lack of knowledge" (Hos. 4:6). It is for that reason, as well as for the even greater reason of honoring the Lord, that regular, systematic, and thorough study of the doctrine in God's Word is imperative for God's people.

John MacArthur

The MacArthur New Testament Commentary series, *2 Timothy* (Moody), © 1987 by John MacArthur. 154-155.

Use the following chart to picture the relationships between the various books of the Bible.

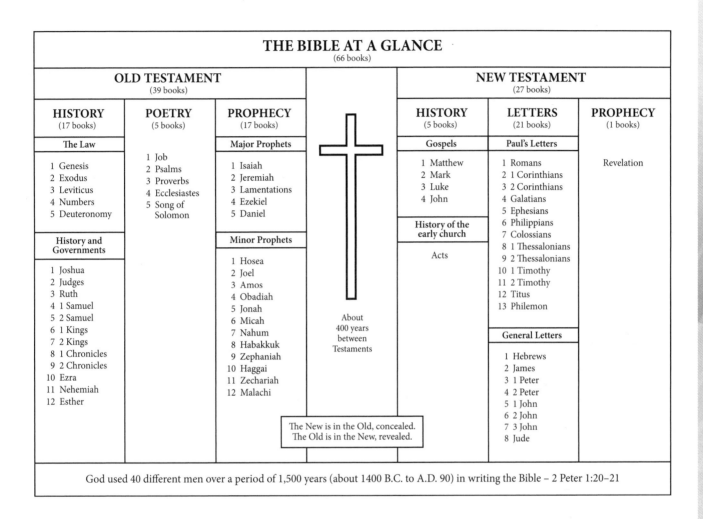

THE BIBLE AT A GLANCE
(66 books)

OLD TESTAMENT (39 books)				NEW TESTAMENT (27 books)		
HISTORY (17 books)	**POETRY** (5 books)	**PROPHECY** (17 books)		**HISTORY** (5 books)	**LETTERS** (21 books)	**PROPHECY** (1 books)
The Law	1 Job	**Major Prophets**		**Gospels**	**Paul's Letters**	Revelation
1 Genesis 2 Exodus 3 Leviticus 4 Numbers 5 Deuteronomy	2 Psalms 3 Proverbs 4 Ecclesiastes 5 Song of Solomon	1 Isaiah 2 Jeremiah 3 Lamentations 4 Ezekiel 5 Daniel		1 Matthew 2 Mark 3 Luke 4 John	1 Romans 2 1 Corinthians 3 2 Corinthians 4 Galatians 5 Ephesians 6 Philippians	
History and Governments		**Minor Prophets**		**History of the early church**	7 Colossians 8 1 Thessalonians 9 2 Thessalonians 10 1 Timothy	
1 Joshua 2 Judges 3 Ruth 4 1 Samuel 5 2 Samuel 6 1 Kings 7 2 Kings 8 1 Chronicles 9 2 Chronicles 10 Ezra 11 Nehemiah 12 Esther		1 Hosea 2 Joel 3 Amos 4 Obadiah 5 Jonah 6 Micah 7 Nahum 8 Habakkuk 9 Zephaniah 10 Haggai 11 Zechariah 12 Malachi	About 400 years between Testaments	Acts	11 2 Timothy 12 Titus 13 Philemon **General Letters** 1 Hebrews 2 James 3 1 Peter 4 2 Peter 5 1 John 6 2 John 7 3 John 8 Jude	

The New is in the Old, concealed.
The Old is in the New, revealed.

God used 40 different men over a period of 1,500 years (about 1400 B.C. to A.D. 90) in writing the Bible – 2 Peter 1:20–21

How the Bible Became Ours

Original Manuscripts

around 1500 B.C. through A.D. 100

Sixty-six distinct works. Some writers unknown.

Manuscripts in original language ⟵ ⟶ Translations into other languages and quotations

A.D. 385–404: The Vulgate, Jerome's Latin translation

▼

700–1000: Various Anglo-Saxon partial translations

▼

1382: Complete translations by John Wycliffe and followers

▼

1525–1535: First printed translation by William Tyndale

▼

1535: Coverdale's translation; 1537: Matthew's; 1539: Taverner's and Great Bible translation; 1560: Geneva Bible; 1568: Bishop's; 1610: Rheim's -Douai

▼

1611: The King James Version

1885: English Revised Version

▼

1901: American Standard Version

▼

More Discoveries → **1947: Dead Sea Scrolls**

▼

1952: Revised Standard Version; 1960: New American Standard Version; 1973: New International Bible
1995: New American Standard Update; 2001: English Standard Version

HOW TO KNOW THE BIBLE

Prepare for Your Assignment

1. Download message #2, "How to Study Scripture," from www.gty.org/fof.

2. Use your notebook to take notes on the message.

3. Work through the questions and tasks on the following pages.

Memorize 2 Timothy 2:15

Be diligent to present yourself approved to God as a workman who does not need to be ashamed, accurately handling the word of truth.

■ It is very obvious, I think, to every Christian, that the Bible is the revelation of God. That God has written His word for us. It is the only rule we have for life. It is the only standard we have for behavior. It is the only authority. There may be other things you learn in life that help you through life but they don't have the authority that God's Word does. When the Bible speaks, that is the voice of God. And it is authoritative and it becomes, then, for us, the standard of life.

There are some Christians who read all kinds of books rather than the Bible. And we say they study about the Bible but they don't study the Bible. The primary thing to do is to study the Word of God. Through it God speaks. Now there are other good books that other men speak through with emphasis on Scripture and application and interpretation but there is no substitute for the Bible. So in the life of every Christian there must be that daily nourishing in the Word of God. It is critical.

John MacArthur

The "how" of learning and applying Scripture to life is something every Christian should know. This lesson covers five ways to make the Bible yours: hearing, reading, studying, memorizing, and meditating. Compare those five methods of learning Scripture to the fingers on your hand. If you hold the Bible with only two fingers, it is easy to lose your grip. But as you use more fingers, your grasp of the Bible becomes stronger.

If a person hears, reads, studies, memorizes, and then meditates on the Bible, his grasp of its truths becomes firm; they are part of his life. As the thumb is needed in combination with any finger to complete your hold, so meditation combined with hearing, reading, studying, and memorizing is essential for a full grasp of God's Word.

HEAR THE BIBLE

So faith comes from hearing, and hearing by the word of Christ. —*Romans 10:17*

READ THE BIBLE

Blessed is he who reads and those who hear the words of the prophecy, and heed the things which are written in it; for the time is near. —*Revelation 1:3*

STUDY THE BIBLE

Now these were more noble-minded than those in Thessalonica, for they received the word with great eagerness, examining the Scriptures daily to see whether these things were so. —*Acts 17:11*

MEMORIZE THE BIBLE

How can a young man keep his way pure? By keeping it according to Your word. With all my heart I have sought You; do not let me wander from Your commandments. Your word I have treasured in my heart, that I may not sin against You. —*Psalm 119:9-11*

MEDITATE ON THE BIBLE

But his delight is in the law of the LORD, and in His law he meditates day and night. He will be like a tree firmly planted by streams of water, which yields its fruit in its season and its leaf does not wither; and in whatever he does, he prospers. —*Psalm 1:2-3*

I. Why to Know the Bible

List five reasons for knowing God's Word.

- ◆ 2 Timothy 2:15 _____
- ◆ 1 Peter 2:2 _____
- ◆ Psalm 119:11 _____
- ◆ Psalm 119:38 _____
- ◆ Psalm 119:105 _____

We study Scripture because it is sufficient.

All Scripture is inspired by God and profitable for teaching, for reproof, for correction, for training in righteousness. —2 Timothy 3:16

II. How to Know the Bible

A. Hear It

"So faith comes from hearing, and hearing by the word of Christ" (Romans 10:17).

1. Whom did Jesus say would be blessed (Luke 11:28)?

_____

2. In proclaiming the Word, what should pastors and teachers do (Nehemiah 8:7–8)?

_____

B. Read It

"Blessed is he who reads and those who hear the words of the prophecy, and heed the things which are written in it; for the time is near" (Revelation 1:3).

1. Write Revelation 1:3 in your own words.

_____

_____

2. To what did Paul ask Timothy to give his attention (1 Timothy 4:13)?

_____

If you do not have a daily reading plan, start with the Gospel of Mark or John. At the rate of two chapters each day, you will complete the New Testament in 19 weeks!

C. Study It

When the apostle Paul left Thessalonica, he came to Berea and shared the gospel with unbelieving Jews. What he found was that they "were more noble-minded than those in Thessalonica, for they received the word with great eagerness, examining the Scriptures daily to see whether these things were so" (Acts 17:11).

Attitudes toward Bible study:

1. According to Acts 17:11, what two traits did the Bereans demonstrate as they received the Word of God?

_____

2. How should we search for wisdom or understanding (Proverbs 2:4)?

_____

Bible study is more than just reading the Bible; it involves careful observation, interpretation, and application. Reading gives you the overall picture, but study helps you think, learn, and apply what you read to your life.

D. Memorize It

"How can a young man keep his way pure? By keeping it according to Your word. . . . Your word I have treasured in my heart, that I may not sin against You" (Psalm 119:9, 11).

1. How did God command Israel to remember His Word?

    a. Deuteronomy 11:18a _____

    b. Deuteronomy 11:19 _____

2. Read Matthew 4:4, 7, 10.

    a. During the three confrontations with Satan, what did Jesus do to overcome His temptations?

    _____

    b. How might you apply this example to your own life?

    _____

    _____

3. Write Psalm 40:8 in your own words.

    _____

It is easier to memorize with a purpose. Understanding the meaning or application of the passage will make memorizing easier.

E. Meditate on It

"How blessed is the man who does not walk in the counsel of the wicked, nor stand in the path of sinners, nor sit in the seat of scoffers! But his delight is in the law of the Lord, and in His law he meditates day and night. He will be like a tree firmly planted by streams of water, which yields its fruit in its season and its leaf does not wither; and in whatever he does, he prospers" (Psalm 1:1–3).

Meditation is prayerful reflection on Scripture with a view toward understanding and application. Give prayerful thought to God's Word with the goal of conforming your life to His will.

1. Meditation on Scripture can be done as you:

    a. Hear the Word preached.

    b. Read the Bible.

    c. Pray about what you are studying.

    d. Reflect on the verses you have memorized.

2. How does mediation assist you (Joshua 1:8)? _____

_____

3. Do you think God's Word can affect your speech and actions? How? (See Luke 6:45.) _____

_____

4. Besides being diligent in learning God's Word, what else should we do in order to understand it (Psalm 119:73, 125)?

_____

III. The Bible Study Process

A. Step 1: Preparation

1. What should we do before we approach the Scriptures (1 Peter 2:1–2)?

_____

2. What should be the content of our prayer as we prepare to study God's Word (Colossians 1:9–10)?

_____

Spend a short time in prayer before each study. Confess any sin and ask the Holy Spirit, "Open my eyes, that I may behold wonderful things from Your law" (Psalm 119:18).

B. Step 2: Observation

"What is taking place in the passage? What do I see?"

1. Ask questions as you read, and *write them down*. Who? What? Where? When?

2. As you observe the passage, look for:

   a. Key words

   b. Key subjects (people, topics)

   c. Commands (particularly verbs)

   d. Warnings

   e. Repeated words or phrases

   f. Comparisons (things that are similar; things that are different)

   g. Questions, answers given

   h. Anything unusual or unexpected

Note: These are just a few examples of things to look for when observing a passage.

Warning: Take your time! Don't give up too soon!

C. Step 3: Interpretation

"What does it mean?"

1. Scripture can be clear. Whom has God given to teach us (1 John 2:27)?

   _____

2. Begin by asking interpretive questions.

   a. What is the importance of:

      (1) A given word (especially verbs)?

      (2) A given phrase?

      (3) Names and titles?

      (4) Dates?

      (5) Others?

   b. What is the meaning of a particular word?

   c. Why did the writer say this?

   d. What is the implication of this word, phrase, or name?

3. To find answers to your interpretive questions, use:

   a. The context—the verses before and after the passage you are studying

   b. Definitions of words

   c. Grammar and sentence structure

   d. Other passages of Scripture

   e. Bible study tools, such as:

      (1) Bible dictionaries

      (2) Concordances

      (3) Bible handbooks

      (4) Bible encyclopedias

      (5) Bible commentaries

4. When interpreting, remember:

   a. That all Scripture will agree. It will not contradict itself.

   b. To let the passage speak for itself in its context. Be careful not to draw conclusions that the author did not intend.

There is only one correct interpretation of any particular passage of Scripture—the author's originally intended meaning.

D. Step 4: Application
"What effect will this have on my life?"

This part of the Bible study process takes the truths that have been observed and seeks to incorporate them into everyday life and practice.

---

1. Once we have heard the Word of God, what should our response be (James 1:22)? _____

_____

2. A simple tool to help you apply what you have learned is to "put on the SPECS." Is there a:

Sin to forsake?

Promise to claim?

Example to follow?

Command to obey?

Stumbling block to avoid?

While there is only one correct *interpretation* of a given passage of Scripture, there are many *applications*.

E. Step 5: Repetition

Bible study is a repetitive process. When studying a verse, steps 2, 3, and 4 are used over and over. *Observe*, then *interpret*, then *apply*. You may choose to do this for each word, phrase, or thought.

The more passes you make through the verse, the deeper its meaning is opened to you.

■ It is necessary to study the Scripture in order to be blessed. I don't know about you, but I like to be happy rather than sad. I'd much rather be happy than miserable. And I know that life is made up of miserable times and happy times. I also know this: The more I study the Word of God, the happier I am no matter what the circumstances are. The Word of God makes me happy.

That's really practical. When you see a miserable person, the first question to ask him is: Have you studied the Bible today? This simple question is the answer to their problem. Psalm 1:1-2 tells us, "How blessed is the man who does not walk in the counsel of the wicked, nor stand in the path of sinners, nor sit in the seat of scoffers! But his delight is in the law of the Lord, and in His law he meditates day and night." That's a happy man. A happy man is somebody who studies the Bible.

John MacArthur

IV. Study Exercise

"But seek first His kingdom and His righteousness; and all these things will be added to you" (Matthew 6:33).

Using Matthew 6:33 and the worksheet:

1. Make as many observations as you can, listing them in the "Observations" column below.

2. Write "Interpretive Questions" about your observations.

3. Write the meaning of your observation in the "Interpretations" column.

4. Once you have completed your observations and interpretations, fill in the "Application" section.

Note: The first six have been supplied as examples.

"But seek first His kingdom and His righteousness; and all these things will be added to you" (Matthew 6:33).

Observations	Interpretive Questions	Interpretations
1. The verse starts with the conjunction *but*.	1. Why does the sentence start with *but*?	1. This verse is linked to the previous verses. Must read Matthew 6:31–32 for context.
2. Key word: *Seek*	2. What does it mean? What action does *seek* require?	2. It means to pursue or search. It is a command.
3. The verb *seek* is in the present tense.	3. What does present tense indicate?	3. I must seek *now*.
4. Note the use of the word *first* following *seek*.	4. What is the importance of *first*?	4. Implies priority. Must seek as a top priority.
5. Next key word is *kingdom*.	5. What does the word *kingdom* signify?	5. It is a sovereign rule or dominion over a specific realm or region.
6. The word *kingdom* is preceded by the personal pronoun *His*.	6. Whose kingdom is identified? To whom does *His* refer?	6. Looking back to verse 32, *His* refers to the "Father." It is God's kingdom.
7.	7.	7.
8.	8.	8.
9.	9.	9.

Observations	Interpretive Questions	Interpretations
10.	10.	10.
11.	11.	11.
12.	12.	12.

Application

Write out one application based on your observations and interpretations. (Refer to SPECS in the "Step 4: Application" section.)

_____

_____

_____

_____

_____

V. Application

Are the 168 hours in your week being invested well? Should you make any changes?

The following table will help you analyze your habits for making the Bible yours. As you fill in the numbers of hours spent per week, pray about setting new goals.

Time in the Word	My Present Program	New Goals and Plans
Hearing the Word		
Reading the Word		
Studying the Word		
Memorizing the Word		

■ It is necessary also to study Scripture in order to help others. You really can't help anybody else unless you know something they need to know. God never put a premium on ignorance. Your ignorance not only makes you unable to help yourself, but it makes you unable to help anybody else. And Christianity is all about helping other people, isn't it? How best can you help a person in trouble? By showing them God's solution to their trouble. How best can you solve a person's problem? By knowing what the Bible says about their problem, and how to handle it.

So you are able to help others when you know the Word of God. For example 2 Timothy 2:2 tells us we are to teach faithful men in order that they may teach others also.

John MacArthur

GOD: HIS CHARACTER AND ATTRIBUTES

Prepare for Your Assignment

1. Download message #3, "God: What Is He Like?" from www.gty.org/fof.

2. Use your notebook to take notes on the message.

3. Work through the questions and tasks on the following pages.

Memorize 1 Chronicles 29:11

Yours, O Lord, is the greatness and the power and the glory and the victory and the majesty, indeed everything that is in the heavens and the earth; Yours is the dominion, O Lord, and You exalt Yourself as head over all.

"Plunge yourself in the Godhead's deepest sea; be lost in His immensity; and you shall come forth as from a couch of rest refreshed and invigorated. I know nothing which can so comfort the soul, so calm the swelling billows of sorrow and grief; so speak peace to the winds of trial, as devout musing upon the subject of the Godhead."

—C. H. Spurgeon on January 7, 1855

I. Introduction

In the religions of today's world, there are many so-called gods and just as many opinions about what God (or god) is like. The Bible, on the other hand, claims to be the revelation of the one true God. The Bible never tries to prove that God exists; it simply states, "In the beginning God…" (Genesis 1:1).

A. How does Psalm 89:7–8 describe God?

_____

_____

B. What statement is made to point to the fact that there is only one God (Isaiah 43:10)?

_____

_____

_____

C. What is it that God will not give to another (Isaiah 42:8)?

_____

II. The Importance of Knowing God

A. Jesus equated knowing God with what (John 17:3)? _____

B. Rather than boasting in wisdom, might, or riches, what one thing does God say a man should boast about (Jeremiah 9:24)?

_____

_____

A right conception of God is basic not only to systematic theology but to practical Christian living as well. . . . I believe there is scarcely an error in doctrine or a failure in applying Christian ethics that cannot be traced finally to imperfect and ignoble thoughts about God.[1] —A. W. Tozer

III. How Can One Know God?

A. What does Jesus say about the means for knowing God (John 14:9–10)?

_____

_____

_____

B. What does Paul say about Christ in Colossians 2:9?

_____

C. The writer of Hebrews says that God has spoken to us in His Son. How is Christ described (Hebrews 1:3)?

_____

_____

IV. God's Attributes

A. What are attributes?

An attribute is a quality or characteristic that is true about someone. Studying God's attributes allows us to have a limited understanding of His Person. Even though some concepts exceed the limits of our comprehension, our ideas concerning God need to be as true as possible.

Father, Son, and Holy Spirit
Holiness
Righteousness and Justice
Sovereignty
Eternality
Immutability
Omniscience
Omnipresence
Omnipotence
Love
Truth
Mercy
Note: These are just a few of God's attributes.

[1] Quote from _The Knowledge of the Holy_ by A.W. Tozer, © 1961 by Aidan Wilson Tozer. Used by permission of Harper-Collins Publishers Inc.

B. God's attributes defined

First look up the following Scripture verses, then write down the part of the verse that best describes the given attribute.

Second, in the Personal Application section, write out how that attribute personally applies to you based on your understanding of the attribute.

1. Holiness

God's attribute of holiness means that He is untouched and unstained by the evil in the world. He is absolutely pure and perfect.

a. Exodus 15:11 _____

_____

b. Psalm 99:9 _____

_____

Because God is holy, we are exhorted to be holy (1 Peter 1:16). We are to be set apart from sin unto God. Our lives are to shine as a reflection of God in an unrighteous world.

Personal Application: _____

_____

_____

_____

2. Righteousness and Justice

Righteousness and *justice* are derived from the same root word in the original language of the New Testament. The meaning is being right or just.

Righteousness designates the perfect agreement between God's nature and His acts. Justice is the way God legislates His righteousness. There is no action that God takes in relation to man that violates any code of morality or justice.

There is no law **above** God, but there is a law **in** God.[2]

---

a. According to Psalm 119:137, God's righteousness is displayed in His _____

[2] Quote from *The Zondervan Pictorial Encyclopedia of the Bible*, Volume 5, ed. Merrill C. Tenney, © 1975, 1976 by The Zondervan Corporation. Used by permission.

b. In Psalm 89:14, righteousness and justice are referred to as _____

_____

How does *your standard* of what is right and just compare with *God's standard*?

Personal Application: _____

_____

_____

_____

_____

_____

_____

_____

3. Sovereignty

The word *sovereign* means chief or highest, supreme in power, or superior in position to all others.

a. Isaiah 46:9–10 _____

_____

b. Isaiah 45:23 _____

The idea of sovereignty is encouraging, for it assures the Christian that nothing is out of God's control and that His plans cannot be thwarted (Romans 8:28).

Personal Application: _____

_____

_____

_____

_____

_____

_____

_____

4. Eternality

Since God is eternal, there has never been a time when He did not exist. He had no beginning and will have no end.

a. Isaiah 44:6 _____

_____

b. Isaiah 43:13 _____

Being eternal, God is not bound by time. Having always existed, He sees the past and the future as clearly as He sees the present. With that perspective, He has a perfect understanding of what is best for our lives. Therefore, we should trust Him with all areas of our lives.

Personal Application: _____

_____

_____

_____

5. Immutability

God never changes in His nature or purpose.

a. Malachi 3:6 _____

_____

b. Hebrews 6:17–18 _____

_____

The Bible contains numerous promises for those who belong to Him. He can be trusted to keep His Word.

Personal Application: _____

_____

_____

_____

_____

_____

6. Omniscience

God knows all things present and future. Nothing takes Him by surprise.

a. Job 34:21 _____

_____

b. Psalm 139:1–6 _____

_____

_____

Since God is omniscient, He knew all our sins (past, present, and future) at the time of our salvation. Yet He still forgave us and received us into His family forever. What does that say about the security of our salvation?

Personal Application: _____

_____

_____

_____

■ At one point in my life I thought about the doctrine of omniscience with anything but confidence. When I was a little kid, my parents used to say, "We may not know what you do, but God does. God sees everything." Remember that beauty? I used to get that. He knows.

As a result, I used to think the doctrine of omniscience was really a bummer. I mean, what a deal. God knew me in ways I wasn't sure I wanted to be known.

Then I studied John 21 and grew up a little bit. And I remembered Peter's conversation with Jesus on the lakeside days after Peter firmly denied knowing Him. Peter kept trying to convince the Lord he loved Him. Remember that? "Lord, I'm telling You, I love You." And the Lord kept asking him and asking. . . . Finally, Peter said, "Lord, look, You know all things, You know that I love You."

What did he appeal to? What doctrine of God? What attribute? Omniscience—omniscience is a great thing. It's not so much that God looks down and spies you out; that's only half of the truth. Do you know that if it weren't for omniscience there are some days when God wouldn't even know you loved Him because it isn't obvious? And if He didn't know everything He wouldn't even know you cared. I suppose in my life there are plenty of days when I am indistinguishable from one of the world's people. Would you agree that is true for your life? How does He know I care? He has to know a lot. He has to know everything. He has to know my heart. Oh, that gives me confidence even when I blow it. My love is still secured because He knows my heart.

John MacArthur

7. **Omnipresence**

God is present everywhere in the universe.

a. Proverbs 15:3 _____

b. Psalm 139:7–12 _____

_____

Since God is everywhere, it is foolish to think we can hide from Him. This also means that a believer may experience the presence of God at all times and know the blessings of walking with Him.

Personal Application: _____

_____

_____

_____

8. **Omnipotence**

God is all-powerful, having more than enough strength to do anything.

a. Jeremiah 32:17 _____

_____

b. Revelation 19:6 _____

God's omnipotence is seen in:

- ♦ His power to create (Genesis 1:1)

- ♦ His preservation of all things (Hebrews 1:3)

- ♦ His providential care for us (Psalm 37:23–24)

"Do not fear, for I am with you; do not anxiously look about you, for I am your God. I will strengthen you, surely I will help you, surely I will uphold you with My righteous right hand" (Isaiah 41:10). What can you learn from Isaiah 41:10 about God's omnipotence?

Personal Application: _____

_____

_____

9. Love

God is love. His love is unconditional; it is not based on the loveliness or merit of the object.

a. John 3:16 _____

_____

b. Romans 5:8 _____

_____

Love expresses itself in action. God is our example. He demonstrated His love for us in sending Jesus to die in our place (2 Corinthians 5:21).

Personal Application: _____

_____

_____

_____

10. Truth

God is the only true God.

a. Psalm 31:5 _____

_____

b. Psalm 117:2 _____

_____

God's truth is above all. He is truthful even if all men are found to be liars. Therefore, His words and His judgments always prevail (Romans 3:4). In light of this, how should you view God's Word and the truths it contains?

Personal Application: _____

_____

_____

_____

11. Mercy

God's great mercy is the practical expression of His compassion to those who have opposed His will.

a. Psalm 145:8–9 _____

_____

b. Psalm 130:3–4 _____

_____

God's great mercy is contrasted with man's sin. His mercy is displayed in our salvation (Ephesians 2:4–5).

Personal Application: _____

_____

_____

_____

V. Application

In light of the attributes of God discussed in this lesson, answer the following questions.

A. How will your prayers be affected? _____

_____

_____

B. How would you respond to a major trial in your life, such as:

1. The death of a close relative (spouse, child)?

_____

_____

_____

2. An accident that leaves you physically disabled?

_____

_____

_____

THE PERSON OF JESUS CHRIST

Prepare for Your Assignment

1. Download message #4, "Christ Above All," from www.gty.org/fof.

2. Use your notebook to take notes on the message.

3. Work through the questions and tasks on the following pages.

Memorize John 1:1, 14

In the beginning was the Word, and the Word was with God, and the Word was God. . . . And the Word became flesh, and dwelt among us, and we saw His glory, glory as of the only begotten from the Father, full of grace and truth.

Jesus Christ is the central figure of all human history. There has never been anyone like Him. He was regarded as a great teacher, a religious leader, a prophet, the Son of God, even God Himself. The claims He made, as well as those that others have made about Him, have propelled Him into the center of endless controversies throughout history.

Pontius Pilate phrased the question perfectly when he asked, "Then what shall I do with Jesus who is called Christ?" (Matthew 27:22). Before you can answer that question, you must first understand who Jesus is. This lesson will introduce Him to you.

I. The God Who Became Man

Jesus Christ came into the world in human flesh. He voluntarily set aside the independent use of His divine attributes and took on the form of a man. He was fully human, a man in every way, except that He was without sin. This is referred to as the "incarnation."

A. What does Philippians 2:6 say about Jesus before He became a man?

_____

_____

B. According to Philippians 2:7, what did Jesus do?

_____

_____

_____

C. Jesus was fully human.

1. Describe Jesus' human growth and development as a youth (Luke 2:40, 52).

_____

_____

2. What was Jesus' response when He was tired (Mark 4:38)? _____

3. What was Jesus' response to lack of food (Luke 4:2)? _____

4. How did Jesus feel after a journey (John 4:6)? _____

5. How did Jesus react when He was grieved (John 11:35)? _____

6. What did Jesus say about Himself (Luke 24:39)? _____

II. The Man Who Is God

Even though Jesus took on the form of a man, He was still fully God. Consider the following marks of deity attributed to Christ.

A. Attributes

Look up the following verses, which describe various attributes of Christ.
Sovereign...Matthew 28:18 Eternal.. 1 John 1:1–2 Unchanging (immutable) .... Hebrews 13:8 All-knowing (omniscient)..Colossians 2:2b–3 Perfect or sinless .... 2 Corinthians 5:21 Holy .... Acts 3:14–15 Truth ....John 14:6

Christ demonstrated His power (omnipotence) in His earthly ministry in the following ways:

1. Matthew 8:23–27: power over _____

2. Luke 4:40: power over _____

3. Luke 4:33–36: power over _____

4. John 11:43–44: power over _____

What additional authority did Jesus claim and exercise (Mark 2:3–12)?

(Hint: see verse 10.)

_____

According to Mark 2:7, who alone can forgive sin? _____

Since Jesus had the authority to forgive sins, and only God can forgive sins, who is Jesus Christ? _____

B. Titles of Deity

1. Matthew 1:23 _____ ("God with us")

2. Philippians 2:10–11 _____ (sovereign)

3. John 8:58 _____ (a title reserved for God; Exodus 3:14)

■ It stands to reason, I believe, that the One who is first in rank in the universe; the One who is the point of reference for history; the One who is the Agent, the Goal, the Forerunner, the Sustainer, the Governor in the sphere of creation; the one who is the Head of the church, and the One who is the beginning, the source, and chief One, the One who is the ranking one of all those resurrected, the One who is the First Fruits, if you will, of them that slept; that One has the right to the title "Preeminent." Wouldn't you say?

John MacArthur

C. Statements of Deity
Write out the key statements.

1. Colossians 2:9 _____

_____

2. Hebrews 1:1–3a _____

_____

_____

3. John 1:1, 14: Jesus Christ ("The Word") is _____

4. Titus 2:13 _____

_____

III. The Christ Who Is Savior

According to John 3:17, Jesus is the Savior of the world. List the following titles that describe God's saving grace.

1. John 1:29 _____

2. John 6:35 _____

3. John 14:6 _____

IV. The King Who Comes to Rule

Jesus is not just a person of the past. He is the destined King of kings and Lord of lords (1 Timothy 6:14–15) who will someday reign over all the earth.

A. **According to Daniel 7:14, what three things has Christ been given?**

1. _____

2. _____

3. _____

B. **What did Jesus tell His followers in Matthew 25:31–32?**

_____

_____

C. **When Christ ascended into heaven 40 days after the resurrection, what were the apostles told (Acts 1:11)?** _____

_____

D. **Describe the return of Jesus Christ (2 Thessalonians 1:7b–10).** _____

_____

_____

_____

V. Application

Christ is:

- ♦ God

- ♦ Savior

- ♦ King/Ruler

A. In light of this, how can you best prepare for His second coming (2 Peter 3:14)?

_____

_____

_____

_____

_____

B. What can you do this week to acknowledge who He is (Revelation 5:11–14)?

_____

_____

_____

_____

_____

THE WORK OF CHRIST

Prepare for Your Assignment

1. Download message #5, "The Suffering Jesus: Our Substitute and Shepherd," from www.gty.org/fof.

2. Use your notebook to take notes on the message.

3. Work through the questions and tasks on the following pages.

Memorize: 1 Corinthians 15:3–4

For I delivered to you as of first importance what I also received, that Christ died for our sins according to the Scriptures, and that He was buried, and that He was raised on the third day according to the Scriptures.

■ Some people think Jesus died as a martyr. They think that Jesus is just a great example of someone who died for a cause. That's the "Jesus Christ Superstar" mentality—that Jesus was a martyr who lived for a good cause and sets a great example of how to be so sold out to a cause that you are willing to die as a martyr. And admittedly, a martyr can be an example of suffering but a martyr cannot be a substitute. A martyr cannot take away my sin by the sacrifice of himself.

John MacArthur

The Scriptures tell us that "He Himself bore our sins in His body on the cross, so that we might die to sin and live to righteousness" (1 Peter 2:24).

I. Man's Need for Christ's Work

A. **According to Romans 3:10–12, every man is guilty of what six things?**

1. _____
2. _____
3. _____
4. _____
5. _____
6. _____

Romans 3:23 sums up the problem: "For all have sinned and fall short of the glory of God."

B. **To what is man a slave (John 8:34)?** _____

C. **What is the result of sin (James 1:15)?** _____

D. **Because we were dead in trespasses and sins, whom did we follow and what kind of children were we (Ephesians 2:1–3)?**

_____

_____

_____

_____

E. **Whose wrath will the "sons of disobedience" experience (Ephesians 5:6)?**

_____

Will God Tolerate Sin?

"Cursed is everyone who does not abide by all things written in the book of the law, to perform them."
—Galatians 3:10

As we studied in lesson 3, God asserts His holiness and demands conformity to that holiness. Man is faced with:

♦ Sin (Romans 3:23)

♦ Having God as his enemy (James 4:4b)

♦ Subjection to the power of Satan (1 John 5:19)

♦ Being helpless to save himself (Romans 5:6)

♦ Death (Romans 6:23)

♦ Condemnation and eternal separation from God (2 Thessalonians 1:9)

II. The Cost of Christ's Work

A. Read Philippians 2:7–8.

1. What are three things Christ did when He came to earth (verse 7)?

    a. _____

    b. _____

    c. _____

2. In what way did Jesus humble Himself (verse 8)? _____

_____

B. What happened to Jesus on earth, according to Isaiah 53:3?

_____

_____

C. Forgiveness of sins requires what (Hebrews 9:22)?

_____

D. What price did Christ pay to redeem us (1 Peter 1:18–19)?

_____

E. What did Jesus cry out on the cross (Matthew 27:46)?

_____

_____

F. What did God do to Jesus while He was on the cross (Isaiah 53:6)?

_____

_____

III. The Provisions of Christ's Work

Jesus Christ came to earth to pay the price for sin. That price was His own life, which He gave voluntarily (John 10:11, 17–18). His sacrifice was the only way to take away sin for all time (Hebrews 9:12).

Describe what Jesus' death accomplished.

A. 1 Peter 3:18 _____

B. Romans 5:10 _____

_____

C. 2 Corinthians 5:21 _____

D. Galatians 1:4 _____

_____

E. Ephesians 1:7 _____

_____

F. Romans 6:6–7 _____

_____

■ At the heart of the church's worship is the beautiful ordinance of the Lord's Table, with which we are very familiar. There at the Lord's Table we take the bread and the cup in remembrance and communion with Christ. At the heart of the Lord's Table is a doctrine and that doctrine is the very core of the Christian Gospel. It is summed up in the words of our Lord who said, "This is My body which is given for you." The essence of the Christian Gospel is that Jesus Christ has done something for us. Most specifically, He died *for* us. That's the point. His death was *for* us. And that is precisely what Peter says in 1 Peter 2:21, "Christ also suffered for you." He suffered for you. It was for us that Christ suffered, that's his point.

John MacArthur

Jesus Christ: The Answer to All Man's Problems Concerning Salvation

Christ's work on the cross and His resurrection are the only solution to man's problems. That is why Peter could proclaim of Jesus Christ:

> "And there is salvation in no one else; for there is no other name under heaven that has been given among men by which we must be saved." —Acts 4:12

Refer to your answers in the first section of this lesson, and note how Christ is the answer to each of man's problems.

Man's Problem	The Solution in Christ	Scripture
A. Guilt before God 1. Not righteous	"Through the obedience of the One the many will be made righteous."	Romans 5:19
2. Not understanding	"The Son of God has come, and has given us understanding."	1 John 5:20
3. Not seeking God	"The Son of Man has come to seek and to save that which was lost."	Luke 19:10
4. Turned away from God	"You were . . . straying . . . but now you have returned to the Shepherd."	1 Peter 2:25
5. All have become useless	"These qualities . . . render you neither useless nor unfruitful in . . . Christ."	2 Peter 1:8
6. No good works	"For we are His workmanship, created in Christ Jesus for good works."	Ephesians 2:10
B. Slavery to sin	"Jesus has set you free from the law of sin and of death."	Romans 8:2
C. Facing death	"He who hears My word, and believes Him who sent Me, has eternal life."	John 5:24
D. Facing the wrath of God	"Justified by His blood, we shall be saved from the wrath of God through Him."	Romans 5:9

IV. The Motive for Christ's Work

A. Why did God save men (John 3:16; Romans 5:8)?

_____

B. What attribute of God is demonstrated in His salvation of men (1 Peter 1:3)?

_____

C. Why does the author call God's mercy great? (Hint: Romans 5:6, 8)

_____

_____

V. The Resolution and Continuation of Christ's Work

Christ's death on Calvary finished His redemptive work for man (John 19:30). But salvation's story does not end there. The grave could not hold Christ; He lives and continues the work He began for us.

A. How was Christ declared to be the Son of God (Romans 1:4)?

_____

B. After Christ made purification of sins, how was He exalted (Hebrews 1:3)?

_____

C. We experience spiritual death through Adam's sin. What benefit do we gain through Christ's resurrection (1 Corinthians 15:21–22)?

_____

The Bible refers to Christ's resurrection as "the first fruits." This is an Old Testament term that speaks of the first fruits of the harvest; these fruits were set apart for the Lord. When used in the New Testament, "first fruits" implies a pledge of more harvest to follow. Therefore, Christ's resurrection holds the promise of resurrection for others also (1 Corinthians 15:20–22; 1 Peter 1:3).

D. Now that we have been drawn to God through Christ, what is Jesus able to do (Hebrews 7:25)? _____

_____

E. What role does Christ hold exclusively (1 Timothy 2:5)? _____

_____

F. When Jesus was going to leave, what did He promise He would do (John 14:3)? _____

_____

_____

VI. Application

When some people are confronted with the reality of who Christ is, they realize they have made a terrible error in what they have believed or how they have lived. They are deeply convicted in their hearts. Consider the example of the men in Jerusalem, whose eyes were opened to the truth.

"Now when they heard this, they were pierced to the heart, and said to Peter and the rest of the apostles, 'Brethren, what shall we do?'" —Acts 2:37

What can you do?

♦ Acknowledge that you have sinned and are not acceptable to God.

♦ Repent and call upon the name of Jesus to save you.

♦ Seek forgiveness through His blood shed for you.

♦ Acknowledge that He is the rightful ruler in your life.

♦ Thank God for His love and grace.

☐ I have repented of my sins and called upon the name of Jesus Christ, believing in Him as Lord and Savior.

☐ I have not received Christ, but I am still earnestly seeking.

SALVATION

Prepare for Your Assignment

1. Download message #6, "Exchanging Living Death for Dying Life," from www.gty.org/fof.

2. Use your notebook to take notes on the message.

3. Work through the questions and tasks on the following pages.

Memorize Ephesians 2:8–10

For by grace you have been saved through faith; and that not of yourselves, it is the gift of God; not as a result of works, so that no one may boast. For we are His workmanship, created in Christ Jesus for good works, which God prepared beforehand so that we would walk in them.

■ John Edie, the nineteenth-century Scottish preacher said, "Men without Christ are death walking. The beauties of holiness do not attract man in his moral insensibility, nor do the miseries of Hell deter him." You can talk about heaven to him, he's not interested. You can talk about hell to him, he's not afraid.

Now this kind of man doesn't need renewal, this kind of man doesn't need repair, this kind of man doesn't need restoration, resuscitation; this kind of man needs resurrection. He needs life, because he's dead.

John MacArthur

How is Christ's redeeming work applied to man? How do we know whether someone is a Christian? God has decreed or ordained a plan of salvation that He has revealed to us in the Bible. In this lesson, we will learn how He saves those who believe.

I. God's Sovereignty in Salvation

A. God's sovereign plan of salvation

1. Read Romans 8:29–30, and write out the progression of how God brings someone to salvation:

Verse 29: whom He _____

He also _____.

Verse 30: whom He _____

He also _____.

Verse 30: whom He _____

He also _____.

Verse 30: whom He _____

He also _____.

2. Read Ephesians 1:4–6 and answer the following:

a. What has been God's plan since before the foundation of the world (verse 4)?

_____

_____

b. What is the purpose of His plan of salvation (verse 6)?

_____

_____

Grace is "God's free and sovereign act of love and mercy in granting salvation through the death and resurrection of Jesus, apart from anything men are or can do, and of His sustaining that salvation to glorification."[1] —John MacArthur

---

[1] Quote from The MacArthur New Testament Commentary series, *Galatians* (Moody), © 1987 by John MacArthur.

B. God implements His plan of salvation

God's Decree to Reveal His Plan

"The mystery which has been kept secret for long ages past, but now is manifested . . . according to the commandment of the eternal God, has been made known to all the nations, leading to obedience of faith."
—Romans 16:25–26

1. What is man's spiritual condition before conversion (Ephesians 2:1)?

_____

2. What does God (the Holy Spirit) do concerning sin (John 16:8)?

_____

3. What is needed before someone can know the truth (2 Timothy 2:25)?

_____

4. Who grants it? _____

5. Read John 1:12–13. Who grants us the right to become children of God (verse 12)?

_____

Notice that this right or privilege is not granted to us because of:

- ◆ Our birth ("of blood")

- ◆ Our own efforts ("will of the flesh")

- ◆ Our own volition ("will of man")

6. Who causes growth in a believer (1 Corinthians 3:6)? _____

7. Who will cause the resurrection to occur (1 Corinthians 6:14)? _____

C. God culminates His plan

1. Look again at Romans 8:29. Into whose image will we be ultimately conformed?

_____

2. What is going to happen to every believer (Philippians 3:20–21)?

_____

_____

3. What is Christ's desire for those who are His (John 17:24)?

_____

II. Conversion

Numbers 21:5–9 records how the children of Israel sinned against God, and so God sent deadly snakes that bit them and caused death. The people realized their sin and asked to be delivered. God instructed Moses to put a fiery bronze serpent on a pole, and when someone was bit, they could look on it and be saved. In a way that illustrates conversion; however, instead of a serpent on a pole, we have the Son of God on a cross.

A. Conviction of sin

1. What has God given people to reveal their sinfulness (Romans 3:20)? _____

2. When the people realized the mistake they made in crucifying Christ, how did they feel in their hearts (Acts 2:36–37)?

_____

B. Repentance from sin

1. Why did the tax collector cry out to God in the temple (Luke 18:13)?

_____

_____

2. Read 2 Corinthians 7:9–10.

   a. What does godly sorrow over sin produce (verse 10)? _____

   b. What does it lead to (verse 10)? _____

Repentance means turning away from sin and turning to God.

C. Turning to Christ

When people who had been bitten by a deadly serpent looked at the serpent on the pole, they were exercising faith in what God said.

1. What promise is given to those who call upon the name of the Lord (Romans 10:13)?

_____

2. Read Romans 10:8–10. Faith is required for salvation.

   a. What must you confess (verse 9)? _____

   b. What must you believe (verse 9)? _____

Faith means trusting in, clinging to, or embracing Jesus Christ, who is the object of our faith.

D. Becoming slaves to righteousness

1. Read Romans 8:1–2.

   a. For the believer in Christ, what is the penalty for sin (verse 1)?

   _____

   b. From what is the believer free (verse 2)? _____ and _____

2. When freed from sin, what does a believer become (Romans 6:18)?

   _____

3. What benefit results (Romans 6:22)?

   _____

   _____

Sanctification is the process of being conformed to the image of Jesus Christ.

III. Evidence of Salvation

Three important evidences of a true believer are: *faith* that works, *love* that labors, and *hope* that endures (1 Thessalonians 1:3–4).

A. Faith that works

1. What reveals genuine faith?

   a. James 2:18 _____

   b. 1 Peter 1:6–7 _____

2. For what did God prepare believers (Ephesians 2:10)? _____

_____

3. Titus 3:8 says that those who have believed in God should do what? Why?

_____

_____

B. Love that labors

1. Besides faith, what else does God take note of in the believer (Hebrews 6:10)?

_____

2. What is the source of love in the life of a believer (Romans 5:5)?

_____

3. What is true of a person who is born of God (1 John 4:7–8)?

_____

4. How does a true believer show love (1 John 3:18–19)?

_____

C. Hope that endures

1. Who did Jesus say will be saved (Matthew 10:22)?

_____

2. What gives us our motivation to endure (1 Timothy 4:10)?

_____

3. Describe the hope that a Christian has.

a. Galatians 5:5 _____

b. 1 Thessalonians 5:8 _____

c. Titus 3:7 _____

D. The three that abide

What three things did Paul notice about the Colossians (Colossians 1:4–5)?

1. _____

2. _____

3. _____

IV. Application

God is sovereign in salvation. The believer is not called to salvation because of his own worthiness but because of God's purpose and grace (Ephesians 1:3–14).

A. Realizing that God has chosen you for salvation, how should you respond (Ephesians 1:4)?

_____

_____

_____

B. How are you exhorted to live (Romans 6:12–13)?

_____

The true believer will be convicted of sin and turn from it. He will be willing to submit to God and follow Christ. A true believer will exhibit:

- ♦ A faith that works

- ♦ A love that labors

- ♦ A hope that endures

Those three qualities are present in every true believer and shape the direction of his life.

Read Psalm 116:16–17. Starting today, what application can you make?

_____

_____

_____

_____

THE PERSON AND MINISTRY OF THE HOLY SPIRIT

Prepare for Your Assignment

1. Download message #7, "Be Filled with the Spirit," from www.gty.org/fof.

2. Use your notebook to take notes on the message.

3. Work through the questions and tasks on the following pages.

Memorize John 14:16

I will ask the Father, and He will give you another Helper, that He may be with you forever.

The Holy Spirit is God. The Bible identifies Him as one of three Persons existing as one God—that is, God the Father, God the Son, and God the Holy Spirit. In this lesson, we will study who the Holy Spirit is and what His presence and ministry are in the believer's life.

I. The Holy Spirit Is a Person

A. Recognized as a person

Personal pronouns such as "He" or "Him" are used to refer to the Holy Spirit rather than "it." List the number of times "He" or "Him" is used in John 14:17 to refer to the Holy Spirit.

_____

B. Attributes of personality

1. **Intellect.** He possesses the ability to know and understand reality.

   a. Romans 8:27: The Holy Spirit has a _____

   b. 1 Corinthians 2:10: The Holy Spirit searches _____

   _____

   c. 1 Corinthians 2:11: The Holy Spirit knows _____

   _____

2. **Emotion.** He possesses the ability to experience emotion.

   Record the emotion attributed to the Holy Spirit in

   Ephesians 4:30. _____

3. **Volition.** He possesses the ability to determine or act decisively.

   List the decision or judgment in which the Holy Spirit demonstrates His attribute of volition.

   a. 1 Corinthians 12:7, 11 _____

   _____

   b. Acts 13:2 _____

   _____

II. The Holy Spirit Is God

A. Attributes

The Holy Spirit: Attributes of Deity		
Omniscient	All-knowing	Isaiah 40:13–14
Omnipresent	Present everywhere	Psalm 139:7
Eternal	Without beginning or end	Hebrews 9:14
Truth	Veracity; integrity	1 John 5:7; John 16:13

B. Statements of deity

1. Write the key statement that shows that the Holy Spirit is God (2 Corinthians 3:17).

   _____

2. According.to Acts 5:3–4, lying to the Holy Spirit is the same thing as lying to _____.

III. The Work of the Holy Spirit

A. According to Psalm 104:30, the Holy Spirit is active in _____.

B. Second Peter 1:20–21 tells us that the Holy Spirit was also active in_____

   _____.

The Holy Spirit Bears Witness of Christ	
Attests that Jesus is the Christ	John 15:26
Will disclose or reveal Christ	John 16:14
Will not speak of Himself	John 16:13

IV. The Ministry of the Holy Spirit in Salvation

One of the most important areas of the Spirit's work is with respect to God's plan of salvation.

A. What special work does the Holy Spirit do (John 16:7–8)?

   _____

B. By whom are sinners born into God's kingdom (John 3:5–8)? _____

C. What work does the Spirit do when a person is saved?

1. Titus 3:5–6 _____

_____

2. 1 Corinthians 12:13 _____

_____

_____

The baptism by the Spirit occurs only once—at the time of salvation.

_____

D. How does the Holy Spirit guarantee a believer's salvation (Ephesians 1:13–14)?

_____

_____

The Sealing of the Holy Spirit[1]

A seal was an ancient device, usually a signet ring or cylinder seal engraved with the owner's name or with a particular design. It was used to seal goods, demonstrate ownership, attest a document's authenticity, or impress an early form of a trademark.

A seal indicates ownership and security. It is the guarantee of future blessings. The presence of the Holy Spirit in our lives is God's promise of our inheritance in the future! What a wonderful assurance.

V. The Ministry of the Holy Spirit in the Believer's Life

A. What is the relationship between the Holy Spirit and the believer (Romans 8:9)?

_____

B. Is it possible to be a Christian and not be indwelled by the Holy Spirit? _____

C. What is another ministry of the Holy Spirit in the life of the believer (1 Corinthians 2:12–13)?

_____

_____

[1] Description of a seal taken from *The Zondervan Pictorial Encyclopedia of the Bible*, Volume 5, ed. Merrill C. Tenney, © 1975, 1976 by The Zondervan Corporation. Used by permission.

D. What exhortations are given to all believers in regard to the Spirit?

    1. Ephesians 4:30 _____

    2. 1 Thessalonians 5:19 _____

    3. Ephesians 5:18 _____

Being Filled with the Holy Spirit

To be filled with the Spirit is to be under His total domination and control. . . . To be filled with the Spirit involves confession of sin, surrender of will, intellect, body, time, talent, possessions, and desires. It requires the death of selfishness and the slaying of self-will. . . . To be filled with God's Spirit is to be filled with His Word. And as we are filled with God's Word, it controls our thinking and action.[2] —John MacArthur

---

E. How does a Christian keep from sinning (Galatians 5:16)?

_____

F. When a believer is filled with the Holy Spirit, he will exhibit the fruit of the Spirit. Read Galatians 5:22–23 and list these qualities below:

    1. _____   6. _____

    2. _____   7. _____

    3. _____   8. _____

    4. _____   9. _____

    5. _____

Are you exhibiting those qualities in your life?

---

[2] Quote from The MacArthur New Testament Commentary series, *Ephesians* (Moody), © 1986 by John MacArthur.

VI. Application

In 1 Corinthians 6:19–20, the apostle Paul writes: "Or do you not know that your body is a temple of the Holy Spirit who is in you, whom you have from God, and that you are not your own? For you have been bought with a price: therefore glorify God in your body."

    A. What significance does that have for you?

_____

_____

_____

_____

    B. What do you need to do to glorify God in your body?

_____

_____

_____

_____

PRAYER AND THE BELIEVER

Prepare for Your Assignment

1. Download message #8, "Praying Unceasingly," from www.gty.org/fof.

2. Use your notebook to take notes on the message.

3. Work through the questions and tasks on the following pages.

Memorize Philippians 4:6–7

Be anxious for nothing, but in everything by prayer and supplication with thanksgiving let your requests be made known to God. And the peace of God, which surpasses all comprehension, will guard your hearts and your minds in Christ Jesus.

The purpose of prayer is to express our submission to the sovereignty of God and our trust in His faithfulness. Prayer is the means by which we express all that is in our hearts to our loving and wise heavenly Father. Prayer is not to give God information, because God knows everything. Prayer brings us into reverent communion with God, worshiping Him and acknowledging Him as the giver of all things.

I. The Nature of Prayer

A. **For the believer, prayer is a learning experience that must be developed into a spiritual discipline.**

1. In Luke 11:1, what did the disciples ask of Jesus? _____

_____

2. Read Romans 8:26.

a. According to the apostle Paul, who assists us in our prayers?_____

b. In light of that, what should we do when we are not sure what to pray for?_____

_____

B. **Prayer is communication with God. Scripture tells us that God is very interested in our personal struggles.**

1. What does Psalm 34:15 say about the Lord? _____

_____

2. What did David bring before God in prayer (Psalm 142:2)?_____

_____

3. How are we encouraged to approach God (Hebrews 4:16)? _____

4. Though we have the privilege of access, what caution does Ecclesiastes 5:2 advise? _____

_____

_____

5. What comfort does 1 Peter 5:6–7 offer believers? _____

_____

C. Prayer is effective. It can change situations—and people. We are encouraged to pray expecting results.

1. For whom did the church pray in Acts 12:5? _____

2. How did God answer their prayers (Acts 12:7)? _____

_____

3. Besides answers, what else does God grant to those who pray (Philippians 4:6–7)?

_____

"The effective prayer of a righteous man can accomplish much." —James 5:16

II. The Practice of Prayer

A. Throughout the Bible, God encourages and commands believers to persevere in prayer.

1. In Luke 18:1, the disciples were taught that they should always pray and not _____

_____

2. What is God's will for believers in Christ Jesus (1 Thessalonians 5:17)?

_____

3. When should believers pray (Ephesians 6:18)? _____

_____

B. In the Bible, you will discover many guidelines to help you develop the practice of prayer.

1. In this parable in Luke 11, what did Jesus teach His disciples to expect if they persisted in prayer (Luke 11:5–10)? _____

_____

■ We can start to understand praying without ceasing by looking at the life of our Lord Himself since He did that. He was obviously in constant communion with the Father. And we see Him in Scripture rising up early to pray. We see Him spending all night in prayer. It must have been an unending and nonstop communion between Himself and the Father. Hebrews tells us that He offered up prayers and supplications with strong crying and tears. That is a fascinating insight. There was an intensity in the prayers of Jesus that is utterly unique, that is utterly amazing. When He prayed on a number of occasions, there was a great agonizing. And we can assume that even though the Scripture does not chronicle for us all the details of all of His praying, it had much of the same kind of intensity as those prayers that we do see and have revealed to us in the text. When the Bible tells us that He went in to the Mount of Olives and prayed all night, there was no doubt an intensity in that kind of praying that we know very little about, if anything.

John MacArthur

2. What does Jesus teach as a requirement for answered prayer (John 15:7)?

_____

3. According to 1 John 5:14, what is our confidence as we pray?

_____

_____

Jesus' Pattern for Prayer: Matthew 6:9–13	
Pray to God	Our Father who is in heaven
Exalt Him, saying	Hallowed be Your name
Submit to Him, praying	Your kingdom come, Your will be done
Look to Him, seeking	Our daily bread (sustenance)
Confess to Him, pleading	Forgive us our debts (sins)
Depend on Him, asking	Do not lead us into temptation
Trust in Him, requesting	Deliver us from evil

C. Look up the following verses and list some of the hindrances to answered prayer.

1. Psalm 66:18 _____

2. James 4:3 _____

3. Isaiah 59:1–2 _____

Four Important Areas of Prayer
Adoration...............Reflect on God Himself. Praise Him for His attributes, His majesty, and His gift of Christ.
Confession ....Admit to God that you have sinned. Be honest and humble. Remember, He knows you and loves you.
Thanksgiving.........Tell God how grateful you are for everything He has given you, even the unpleasant things. Your thankfulness will help you see His purposes.
Supplication ....Make specific requests. Pray first for others and then for yourself.
Notice that the first letters of these four words form the word "ACTS." You can use this acronym as a guide to maintain balance as you pray.

III. The Struggle of Prayer

A. Prayer can be hard work, but that should not keep us from praying, even when it requires sacrifice.

1. How long did Jesus pray before He selected the 12 apostles (Luke 6:12)?

_____

2. Describe the intensity of Jesus as He prayed in anticipation of the cross (Luke 22:44).

_____

3. What should believers be careful to do when we devote ourselves to prayer (Colossians 4:2)?

_____

B. Even when we are frustrated or discouraged, we can still approach God in prayer.

1. Why was David discouraged in Psalm 13:1–2? _____

_____

2. What was David's complaint in Psalm 22:2? _____

_____

C. Prayer is governed by God's sovereignty, and His purpose determines His answer to our prayers.

    1. Read 2 Corinthians 12:7–9.

        a. What did Paul pray for? _____

        b. How many times did he pray for it? _____

        c. Did he receive what he asked for? Why or why not? _____

        _____

    2. Read Mark 14:35–36.

        a. What did Jesus ask of the Father concerning His "hour" of suffering?

        _____

        b. But what was He willing to do? _____

        _____

IV. Application

Compose a simple prayer, following the ACTS model on page 62.

_____

_____

_____

_____

_____

_____

_____

_____

_____

_____

_____

Surrender your requests to God's wise and loving plan, acknowledging
your willingness to receive His answer with thankfulness.

The Church: Fellowship and Worship

Prepare for Your Assignment

1. Download message #9, "The Body of Christ," from www.gty.org/fof.

2. Use your notebook to take notes on the message.

3. Work through the questions and tasks on the following pages.

Memorize Hebrews 10:24–25

And let us consider how to stimulate one another to love and good deeds, not forsaking our own assembling together, as is the habit of some, but encouraging one another; and all the more as you see the day drawing near.

I. The Universal Church

"The Church is not a physical building, but a group of believers; not a denomination, sect, or association, but a spiritual Body. The Church is not an organization, but a communion, a fellowship that includes believers."[1] —John MacArthur

   A. Read Colossians 1:18 and Ephesians 5:23.

      1. What is Christ's position in the church? _____

      2. How is the church described? _____

   B. At what cost did Christ purchase the church (Acts 20:28)? _____

   C. How does a person become a member of the Body of Christ?

      1. Colossians 3:15: We are _____ into the body.

      2. 1 Corinthians 12:13: We are _____ into the body.

II. The Local Church

The New Testament describes how believers came together in small groups to worship Christ, receive instruction from the Scriptures, meet one another's needs, pray, and evangelize.

   A. The local church illustrated

      1. Where did the believers meet before they had church buildings (Romans 16:5; 1 Corinthians 16:19)?

      _____

      2. On what day of the week did they meet (Acts 20:7)?

      _____

[1] Quote taken from *Body Dynamics* by John MacArthur, © 1982 by Scripture Press. Used by permission.

3. List four things to which the early church was devoted (Acts 2:42):

a. _____   c. _____

b. _____   d. _____

B. The local church organized

1. Gifted Men

According to Ephesians 4:11–12, God gave four types of gifted men to the church. List them:

_____   _____

_____   _____

God gave these gifted men to the church to equip the saints for what purposes (verse 12)?

_____

_____

2. Elders/Overseers

The qualifications of an elder or overseer are stated in 1 Timothy 3:1–7 and Titus 1:6–9.

a. What are the two major responsibilities of an elder (1 Peter 5:1–2)?

(1) _____

(2) _____

b. What is the responsibility of believers to the elders (Hebrews 13:17)?

_____

Why? _____

_____

3. Deacons

The word *deacon* means "servant." The deacons are to minister to the needs of the flock under the direction of the elders of the church. The qualifications of deacons are stated in 1 Timothy 3:8–13.

4. Members of the Body

a. What does Hebrews 10:25 warn believers not to neglect?

_____

b. Hebrews 13:7 instructs us concerning those who teach us God's Word. What should be our response? (Select the correct answer).

☐ We should encourage others to come and hear them.

☐ We should not hope to have the kind of faith they have.

☐ We should observe their godly lives and follow their example of faith.

c. How should we act toward other members of the Body (1 Corinthians 12:25)?

_____

5. How should those who are appointed to preach and teach be supported?

a. 1 Corinthians 9:14 _____

_____

b. Galatians 6:6 _____

_____

III. Fellowship

The Bible uses the Greek word *koinonia* to describe fellowship within the Body of Christ. That word means "participation with others in a common purpose." The Latin equivalent is *communion*, pointing to the communion that is shared with other believers as well as with God.

A. Unity within the church

1. What is God's desire for every local church (1 Corinthians 1:10)?

_____

2. Read Ephesians 4:2–3.

What will promote unity (verse 2)? _____

_____

What is our responsibility (verse 3)? _____

_____

3. Read Philippians 2:1–4. What is the key to maintaining unity within the body (verse 3)?

_____

_____

B. Fellowship with God and with other believers ✓

Scripture is clear that the believer enjoys fellowship with:

1. God the Father (1 John 1:3)

2. God the Son (1 John 1:3)

3. The Holy Spirit (2 Corinthians 13:14)

4. Other believers (1 John 1:7)

However, with whom is true fellowship not possible (2 Corinthians 6:14–15)? _____

C. Fellowhip involves ministering to other believers

1. Fellowship within the Body of Christ involves sharing in each other's lives. According to each verse below, how should Christians minister to one another?

   ♦ Romans 14:19 _____

   ♦ Galatians 5:13 _____

   ♦ Galatians 6:2 _____

   ♦ James 5:16 _____

2. What has God given to each Christian to help him or her minister to others within the church (1 Peter 4:10–11)?

   _____

IV. Worship

The English word *worship* originally was spelled "worthship," meaning to acknowledge the worth of someone or something. We worship when we give honor to God for who He is. Worship acknowledges God's Person, nature, attributes, and works. It stems from a grateful heart and renders adoration, devotion, and submission to God.

A. God seeks genuine worshipers.

Read John 4:23–24. How are we to worship God (verse 24)? _____

_____

If we are to worship God in truth (not in error), we must seek to know Him by learning about His attributes and actions.

_____

B. We worship God because only He is worthy of our highest devotion. ✓

Read Revelation 4:10–11 and answer the following questions.

1. What is God worthy to receive? _____

2. Why? _____

C. Worshiping God involves praise. ✓

How did the psalmist say God should be worshiped (Psalm 66:4)? _____

D. Worshiping God involves reverence. ✓

1. What did Moses do when he worshiped God (Exodus 34:8)?

_____

2. How is reverence for God revealed in the following verses?

a. Exodus 34:8 _____

b. Luke 7:1–7 _____

c. Revelation 1:17 _____

"O come, let us sing for joy to the Lord, let us shout joyfully to the rock of our salvation. Let us come before His presence with thanksgiving, let us shout joyfully to Him with psalms. For the Lord is a great God and a great King above all gods, in whose hand are the depths of the earth, the peaks of the mountains are His also. The sea is His, for it was He who made it, and His hands formed the dry land. Come, let us worship and bow down, let us kneel before the Lord our Maker." —Psalm 95:1–6

V. Ordinances of the Church

The Ordinance of Baptism

Baptism was instituted by our Lord and practiced by early believers. As explained in the Scriptures, baptism was a declaration of the believer's identification with Jesus Christ in His death, burial, and resurrection. Clearly, baptism was practiced by the early church, and therefore, we believe this ordinance should be practiced by the church today.

Why baptize?
We baptize because:
- Baptism was commanded by our Lord—Matthew. 28:19.
- Baptism was practiced by the early church—Acts 2:41; 8:26–39; 10:44–48; 16:31–33; 18:8.

Who should be baptized?
In the Scriptures we find examples of disciples (or followers) of Christ, believers, and those who had received the Holy Spirit being baptized:

- Disciples (or followers of Christ)—Matthew 28:19.
- Believers—Acts 2:41; Acts 8:30–38; Acts 16:33–34.
- Those who have received the Holy Spirit—Acts 10:44–48.

Therefore, we conclude that those who have personally confessed Jesus Christ as their Savior and Lord (i.e., Christians) should be baptized.

What does baptism mean?
Baptism is a declaration of the believer's identification with Christ:

- Identification with Christ in His death—Romans 6:3
- Identification with Christ in His burial—Romans 6:4a
- Identification with Christ in His resurrection—Romans 6:4b

Baptism is an acknowledgment "that our old self was crucified with Him" (Romans 6:6) and a profession that henceforth we "might walk in newness of life" (Romans 6:4b).

How should we baptize?
We believe that a person should be baptized by being fully immersed in water:

- The word *baptism* was transliterated from the word *baptizo* meaning to "make fully whelmed; to dip or to sink".
- Baptism took place where there was *much water*—John 3:23
- When they baptized they went *down into the water* (Acts 8:38) and *came up from the water* (Matthew 3:16).

Also, when baptizing by immersion, the picture of going down into the water and coming up out of the water symbolizes the believer's identification with Christ's death, burial, and resurrection.

Have you confessed Jesus Christ as Lord and Savior? _____

Have you been baptized as a believer? _____

The Ordinance of Communion

The Lord's Supper, or Communion, is one of two ordinances given to the church by Jesus Christ (the other being baptism). The Lord's Supper is an act of remembrance of Christ's death.

Read 1 Corinthians 11:23–26 and fill in the blanks below.

1. The bread is in remembrance of _____.

2. The cup is in remembrance of _____.

3. Every time you partake in Communion, you proclaim the Lord's death (1 Corinthians 11:26). In light of that truth, what is the warning stated in 1 Corinthians 11:27–30?

_____

_____

_____

VI. Application

A. Are you a member of the Body of Christ?

_____

B. Are you a member of a local assembly of Christians?

_____

C. What have you learned from this study to improve your worship of God?

_____

_____

_____

_____

SPIRITUAL GIFTS

Prepare for Your Assignment

1. Download message #10, "Miracles, Healing, and Tongues," from www.gty.org/fof.

2. Use your notebook to take notes on the message.

3. Work through the questions and tasks on the following pages.

Memorize 1 Corinthians 12:7

But to each one is given the manifestation of the Spirit for the common good.

God gives spiritual gifts to believers for the purpose of ministry within the church. The English term comes from two Greek words, *charismata* and *pneumatika*. The root of *charismata* is *charis*, which means "grace" and speaks of something undeserved or unearned. The second word, *pneumatika*, means "spirituals," or things given by the Spirit of God. In this lesson, you will look at various spiritual gifts and how they should be used in the Body of Christ.

I. The Nature of Spiritual Gifts

A. Who is the source of spiritual giftedness?

1. 1 Corinthians 12:11 _____

2. 1 Corinthians 12:28 _____

B. Who possesses spiritual giftedness (1 Peter 4:10)?

_____

C. What is the purpose of spiritual gifts?

1. 1 Corinthians 12:4–7 _____

_____

2. 1 Corinthians 14:12 _____

_____

3. 1 Peter 4:10–11 _____

_____

_____

II. The Provision of Spiritual Gifts

A. Spiritual gifts are referred to in Scripture.
List them below:

1. Romans 12:6–8

_____ _____ _____

_____ _____ _____

_____

2. 1 Corinthians 12:8–10

_____ _____ _____

_____ _____ _____

_____ _____ _____

3. 1 Corinthians 12:28b (second half of verse)

_____ _____ _____

_____ _____

B. Understanding the gifts—temporary gifts

For a better understanding of how the spiritual gifts function, we have classified the gifts into two categories: temporary (special) and permanent.

The Holy Spirit gave temporary gifts to confirm the testimony of the apostles and prophets. These gifts were prevalent in the early church but ceased to be evident as the church became established.

1. Miracles

This gift is the ability to do "wonders" and "signs." Christ performed many miracles, as recorded in Scripture. Paul used this gift to affirm his apostleship, as described in 2 Corinthians 12:12.

2. Healing

Peter had this gift (see Acts 3:6–8; 5:15–16), which affirmed his message and helped to establish the foundation for the church.

3. Tongues and interpretation of tongues

This gift is manifested by the speaking of a language unknown to the speaker (see Acts 2:1–11). This gift had to be accompanied by the gift of interpretation (1 Corinthians 14:27–28).

C. Understanding the gifts—permanent gifts

The Holy Spirit gave gifts for the building up of the church. These were prevalent in the early church and still are in the church today.

1. Prophecy

To prophesy is to preach or to tell forth or declare the Scripture. Prophecy does not necessarily mean to foretell the future.

2. Teaching

This gift is the ability to teach the Word of God and help the hearers to understand the Scriptures as the Author intended.

3. Faith

This gift is a consistent, enabling faith that truly believes God in the face of overwhelming obstacles and human impossibilities, and for great things. John MacArthur calls this the "gift of prayer" because the gift is primarily expressed toward God through prayer.

4. Wisdom

This is the ability to apply wisdom, gained from spiritual insight, to believers; knowing what is right and what is wrong, applied knowledge.

5. Knowledge

This is an understanding of the facts of Scripture. From the human perspective, it is scholarship or the ability to know the truths of Scripture both broadly and deeply.

6. Discernment

Discernment is the ability to tell which things are from the Spirit and which are not, distinguishing truth from error. This gift serves as protection for the church.

7. Mercy

This is the ability to show deep compassion to those who have spiritual, physical, or emotional needs.

8. Exhortation

Exhortation is the ability to encourage and motivate. A person with this gift can come alongside another to comfort him with love, to encourage him to a deeper spiritual commitment and growth, or to exhort him to action. This is the gift that qualifies people to exercise a counseling ministry in the body.

9. Giving

This gift is a direct reference to the material ministry of giving food, clothes, money, houses, etc., in response to the needs of the church.

10. Administration/Leadership

This gift is the ability to oversee the flock. This gift should be exhibited by pastors and elders, as well as leaders of missionary societies, youth ministries, evangelistic associations, etc.

11. Helps

This gift is the ability to aid in a time of need or bear one another's burdens as the situation arises.

12. Service

The gift of service is working for the Body of Christ in areas of physical ministry, such as serving food or performing maintenance.

III. The Exercise of Spiritual Gifts

A. State the principle(s) expressed in Romans 12:6–8.

_____

_____

B. Read 1 Corinthians 13:1–7 and answer the following questions:

1. How can your gifts be abused and without benefit (verses 1–3)?

_____

2. Since your spiritual giftedness is to be exercised in love, what are some guidelines that will ensure the profitability of your gifts?

List 15 guidelines (verses 4–7).

a. _____   i. _____

b. _____   j. _____

c. _____   k. _____

d. _____   l. _____

e. _____   m. _____

f. _____   n. _____

g. _____   o. _____

h. _____

C. First Corinthians 12 reveals the importance of each spiritual gift within the Body of Christ. According to 1 Corinthians 12:25, what should your attitude be in the use of your spiritual giftedness?

_____

_____

D. Read Ephesians 4:11–16. What causes the growth of the Body of Christ (verse 16)?

_____

_____

IV. Application

Discovery of Your Giftedness
Each member of the body is commanded to minister in many of the gifted areas, whether he possesses that particular gift or not. For example, all Christians are to function in the following areas: Faith .... 2 Corinthians 5:7 Wisdom .... James 1:5 Knowledge .... 2 Timothy 2:15 Exhortation .... Hebrews 10:25 Giving .... 2 Corinthians 9:7 Care for one another (helps) .... 1 Corinthians 12:25

The Bible does not explicitly explain how to determine one's spiritual giftedness. However, you can begin by being obedient in the areas mentioned above. Look for open doors, and pray for opportunities to serve. Seek the counsel of other believers; they may be more aware of your gifts than you are.

In order to discover your giftedness in the body and in submission to the elders of your church, in what areas would you be willing to serve?

1. _____

2. _____

3. _____

Each of us needs to exercise his or her giftedness in ministry for the common good of the church.

"As each one has received a special gift, employ it in serving one another as good stewards of the manifold grace of God." —1 Peter 4:10

Evangelism and the Believer

Prepare for Your Assignment

1. Download message #11, "Fishing for Men," from www.gty.org/fof.

2. Use your notebook to take notes on the message.

3. Work through the questions and tasks on the following pages.

Memorize 1 Peter 3:15

But sanctify Christ as Lord in your hearts, always being ready to make a defense to everyone who asks you to give an account for the hope that is in you, yet with gentleness and reverence.

The word *evangelism* brings many thoughts to mind. Some people think of tents and famous speakers; others envision weekly "visitation" and the terror of "witnessing." This lesson will introduce the biblical concept of evangelism and the role the believer plays.

I. The Call to Evangelism

A. According to Mark 16:15, what were the disciples to do?

_____

_____

B. What are the three aspects of making disciples, according to Matthew 28:19–20?

1. _____

2. _____

3. _____

C. What did Jesus say should be proclaimed to all the nations (Luke 24:46–47)?

_____

_____

_____

_____

D. What was Paul to tell all people (Acts 22:15)?

_____

_____

_____

■ First John 4 tells us that we only love God because He first loved us. And John 3:16 tells us that "God so loved the world, that He gave." The greatest work in the heart of God, the greatest concern in the mind of God is evangelism. Winning the lost is God's great concern. It is also Christ's great concern. Luke 19:10 says, "For the Son of Man has come to seek and to save that which was lost." The work of winning the lost is God's concern and Christ's concern, and also the greatest concern of the Holy Spirit, for it is the Holy Spirit who comes, according to John 16, to convict men of sin and righteousness and of judgment. It is the Holy Spirit who comes upon the church and after we have received the Holy Spirit, we are made witnesses, Jesus said, unto Him, "in Jerusalem, and in all Judea and Samaria, and even to the remotest part of the earth." The great concern of God is evangelism. The great concern of Christ is evangelism. The great concern of the Spirit is evangelism, saving the lost.

John MacArthur

II. The Good News of Evangelism: The Gospel

A. According to 1 Corinthians 15:3–4, what is the good news that Paul preached?

1. _____

2. _____

3. _____

B. Of what did Paul say he was not ashamed (Romans 1:16)? _____

C. Why? _____

III. The Essentials of Evangelism

A. What must someone believe about Jesus Christ for salvation?

1. John 1:1 _____

2. John 14:6 _____

3. Acts 4:12 _____

B. The following are key verses in sharing the gospel message. Look up each verse and briefly summarize the main point.

1. Romans 3:23 _____

_____

2. Romans 6:23 _____

3. Romans 5:8 _____

_____

4. 1 Peter 2:24 _____

_____

5. Romans 10:9 _____

_____

6. John 1:12 _____

_____

Most people do not understand these truths:
Man cannot save himself .... Mark 10:26–27
God is holy and righteous, and He hates sin .... Psalm 5:4–5
Jesus Christ is God .... Colossians 2:9
Christ's death on the cross was for our sins .... 1 Peter 3:18
Christ offers heaven as a free gift of God .... Romans 6:23

IV. Strategy for Evangelism

A. Witness by your life

1. What kind of life should we live, and how should we appear to the world (Philippians 2:14–15)?

_____

_____

_____

_____

Others will see your Redeemer through your redeemed life.

_____

2. Read Matthew 5:16.

a. What do people notice that makes a Christian's life shine? _____

b. What will be the result? _____

3. According to Colossians 4:6, how should you speak to others?

_____

_____

B. Pray

1. As Paul prayed for others, what was on his heart (Romans 10:1)?

_____

2. For what requests did Paul ask the Colossians to pray (Colossians 4:3–4)?

_____

_____

3. When speaking the Word of God to others, especially in threatening situations, what should we ask God to give us (Acts 4:29)?

_____

_____

"First of all, then, I urge that entreaties and prayers, petitions and thanksgivings, be made on behalf of all men . . . This is good and acceptable in the sight of God our Savior, who desires all men to be saved and to come to the knowledge of the truth."

—1 Timothy 2:1, 3–4

C. Use God's Word

1. What will God's Word do (Hebrews 4:12)?

_____

_____

2. How did Paul use Scripture in witnessing (Acts 17:2–3)?

_____

_____

3. What are the Scriptures able to do (2 Timothy 3:15)?

_____

_____

We must be ready to speak of Christ in any situation. We must know the essentials of the gospel. We must have confidence in God and His Word.

"Always being ready to make a defense . . . to give an account for the hope that is in you."

—1 Peter 3:15

Then pray and look for opportunities!

V. Application

List several people whom you want to reach for Christ. Pray regularly for those people, and prepare for the opportunity to share the Word of God with them. Allow God to do His convicting work, and trust Him.

1. _____

2. _____

3. _____

4. _____

5. _____

Remember, exemplify Christlikeness.

Witness to people with your life, and your message will be more clearly understood!

OBEDIENCE

Prepare for Your Assignment

1. Download message #12, "Love and Obedience," from www.gty.org/fof.

2. Use your notebook to take notes on the message.

3. Work through the questions and tasks on the following pages.

Memorize 1 John 2:3–4

By this we know that we have come to know Him, if we keep His commandments. The one who says, "I have come to know Him," and does not keep His commandments, is a liar, and the truth is not in him.

■ We are called, I believe, to love the Lord Jesus Christ, to love Him with a whole soul, whole heart, whole mind, and whole strength kind of love. And we would say we do! But I look at our society; I look at the church, and I don't see that same kind of devotion, that same kind of commitment, that same kind of abandonment to the priorities that are the divine priorities. I see us defused into a myriad of options, giving equal weight or even greater weight to some of the passing things in favor of some of the eternal things.

John MacArthur

Obedience is the expected response of a Christian to his Lord. But obedience is more than following a set of rules. In this lesson, we will study what it means to be obedient, areas of obedience, and some results of obedience.

I. The Call to Obedience

"As obedient children . . . like the Holy One who called you, be holy yourselves also in all your behavior." —1 Peter 1:14–15

A. The Call to Obey God's Commands

1. In John 14:15, Jesus said, "If you love Me, you will

_____."

2. What is expected of those who hear God's Word (James 1:22)? _____

_____

B. The Call to Follow Christ

1. What is required of a person who follows Jesus (Luke 9:23)?

a. _____

b. _____

c. _____

2. How did Jesus set the example for us when suffering for His obedience to God (1 Peter 2:20–23)?

_____

_____

_____

_____

C. The Call to Submission

_____

"Do you not know that when you present yourselves to someone as slaves for obedience, you are slaves of the one whom you obey, either of sin resulting in death, or of obedience resulting in righteousness?"
—Romans 6:16

_____

How should we present ourselves to God (Romans 12:1)?

_____

_____

II. Obedience Marks a True Believer

A. Look at 1 John 2:3–4 (the memory verse).

1. What does obeying the Word of God demonstrate?

_____

2. What does continuous disobedience to the Word of God indicate?

_____

B. What characterizes the true believer as one who will enter the kingdom of heaven (Matthew 7:21)?

_____

_____

"But whoever keeps His word, in him the love of God has truly been perfected. By this we know that we are in Him." —1 John 2:5

_____

III. Examples of Disobedience

A. Read 1 Samuel 15:16–23. Instead of being completely obedient to God's command, King Saul substituted his own way of worship and excused his disobedience.

1. What was Samuel's reply? How did he compare obedience and sacrifice (verse 22)?

_____

2. To what are stubbornness and rebellion compared (verse 23)?

_____

3. What did Saul's disobedience cost him (verse 23)?

_____

B. Consider Zechariah 7:8–14.

1. How did the people react to God's instruction (verses 11–12)?

_____

2. How did it affect their prayers (verse 13)?

_____

3. What was the result (verse 14)?

_____

_____

IV. Examples of Obedience

The Old Testament contains numerous examples of obedience. Notice the Old Testament heroes of faith and obedience listed in Hebrews 11.

A. Abraham's obedience

1. What were two of Abraham's great acts of obedience?

a. Genesis 12:1–4; Hebrews 11:8 _____

_____

b. Genesis 22:1–12 _____

_____

2. Because Abraham obeyed God, what three things did God promise to Abraham's son (Genesis 26:2–5)?

a. _____

b. _____

c. _____

B. Christ's Example of Obedience

1. What was Christ's primary concern on earth (John 4:34)?

_____

2. Even when facing the cross, what was Christ's attitude (Luke 22:42)?

_____

3. To what extent was Jesus willing to be obedient (Philippians 2:8)?

_____

V. The Promise and Blessings of Obedience

A. List some blessings that are promised to us if we obey God's commandments.

1. John 15:10 _____

2. John 15:14 _____

3. 1 John 3:22 _____

B. To what does Jesus compare the life of a person who hears and obeys His Word (Matthew

7:24–27)? _____

VI. Areas of Obedience

A. What are all Christians to be taught concerning Christ's commands (Matthew 28:20)?

_____

B. Read each verse below. Fill in who is to be obedient to whom and why.

1. Colossians 3:20

a. Who? _____ To whom? _____

b. Why? _____

2. Ephesians 5:22–24

a. Who? _____ To whom? _____

b. Why? _____

_____ (Note Ephesians 5:25–32.)

3. Ephesians 6:5–8

    a. Who? _____ To whom? _____

    b. Why? _____

4. Hebrews 13:17

    a. Who? _____ To whom? _____

    b. Why? _____

    _____

5. Romans 13:1

    a. Who? _____ To whom? _____

    b. Why? _____

    _____

C. What should a wife do if her husband is an unbeliever (1 Peter 3:1)?

_____

_____

D. What if a servant (or employee) has an "impossible" employer? What should that servant or employee do (1 Peter 2:18–19)?

_____

_____

VII. Our Attitude toward Obedience

We must remember that all our good works apart from faith are like a filthy garment (Isaiah 64:6). Obedience without genuine faith avails nothing. Our obedience must grow out of a heart of sincere faith toward God.

A. What was the basis of all Abraham's obedience (Hebrews 11:8)? _____

B. Read the parable of the two sons (Matthew 21:28–32). Which son had the better attitude? Why?

_____

C. Using Peter as our example, how should we respond when God's Word seems contrary to our own judgment (Luke 5:4–7)?

_____

D. Read Ephesians 6:6.

1. How should we view ourselves in relation to Christ? _____

2. What should be our attitude in doing the will of God? _____

_____

_____

"So you too, when you do all the things which are commanded you, say, 'We are unworthy slaves; we have done only that which we ought to have done.'"—Luke 17:10

_____

VIII. Application

A. **What does it mean to "present your bodies a living and holy sacrifice, acceptable to God" (Romans 12:1)?**

_____

_____

_____

B. **What have you learned about the consequences of disobedience?**

_____

_____

_____

C. **In what areas of your life does God want greater obedience?**

_____

_____

_____

GOD'S WILL AND GUIDANCE

Prepare for Your Assignment

1. Download message #13, "Knowing and Doing God's Will," from www.gty.org/fof.

2. Use your notebook to take notes on the message.

3. Work through the questions and tasks on the following pages.

Memorize Ephesians 5:17

So then do not be foolish, but understand what the will of the Lord is.

God is sovereign and has a purpose for all of His creation. He has a plan or "will" for each of us, though we often make His will more difficult to respond to than it really is. In this lesson we will explore God's will and how we are guided into it.

I. God's Will

The Bible portrays two aspects of God's will: sovereign will and commanded will. In God's sovereignty, He has a plan that covers all aspects of creation and time. He also has a commanded will that He legislates to His people.

A. The meaning of God's will

1. God's sovereign will

God's sovereign will involves His ultimate, complete control over everything. Nothing happens that is not in God's plan. History is really the unfolding of God's purposes, which happen exactly as He planned.

Look up each of the following verses, and write out the key thought about God's sovereign will.

a. Isaiah 14:24 _____

_____

_____

b. Ephesians 1:11b _____

_____

_____

"I am God, and there is no one like Me. . . . My purpose will be established, and I will accomplish all My good pleasure."
—Isaiah 46:9–10

2. God's commanded will

God's commanded will is revealed throughout the Bible as laws or principles. It is that aspect of His will to which men are held accountable.

a. According to the Great Commission (Matthew 28:20), what are new believers to be taught?

_____

b. God gave two great commandments. List them below.

Matthew 22:37 _____

_____

Matthew 22:39 _____

_____

B. The nature of God's will

God's sovereign will and commanded will are better understood in light of their respective characteristics.

SOVEREIGN WILL	COMMANDED WILL
1. Secret; known only to God except as revealed through history or revelation	1. Revealed in the Bible
2. Cannot be resisted or thwarted	2. Can be resisted or disobeyed
3. Encompasses both good and evil (sin)	3. Involves only that which is good and holy
4. Comprehensive; controls all aspects of life, time, and history	4. Specific; provides principles for living
5. The believer is not commanded to know or discover what God has not revealed	5. Believers are exhorted to know, understand, and obey all that God has revealed

Study the table above. Test your understanding of God's *sovereign will* and His *commanded will*.

Write out the part of the verse that conveys God's will.

Check the appropriate box.

		Sovereign Will	Commanded Will
1.	Philippians 2:13	☐	☐
2.	1 Thessalonians 4:3	☐	☐
3.	2 Corinthians 6:14	☐	☐
4.	Matthew 7:21	☐	☐
5.	Philippians 1:6	☐	☐
6.	Jeremiah 29:11	☐	☐

C. Response to God's will

1. How should we respond to God's sovereign will?

a. Proverbs 3:5–6 _____

_____

b. 1 Peter 4:19 _____

_____

c. James 4:13–15 _____

_____

2. How should we respond to God's commanded will?

a. Ephesians 5:17 _____

_____

b. Deuteronomy 29:29 _____

_____

c. Deuteronomy 11:1 _____

_____

God Instructs; We Obey

"Good and upright is the Lord; therefore He instructs sinners in the way. He leads the humble in justice, and He teaches the humble His way. All the paths of the Lord are lovingkindness and truth to those who keep His covenant and His testimonies." —Psalm 25:8–10

II. Guidance

Because of His great love, God has predestined, called, justified, and will glorify all believers. He also guides us.

A. Meaning of guidance

Guidance is God's active role in our lives, accomplishing His purposes.

Note the following words used in the Bible to describe guidance. Write down how the verse conveys the meaning of each word.

1. *Lead* (to shepherd; to bear or carry)

a. Psalm 78:52 _____

_____

b. Psalm 139:24 _____

_____

2. *Guide* (to show; to help understand)

a. Psalm 23:3 _____

_____

b. Psalm 73:24 _____

_____

3. **Direct** (to establish or prepare; to make straight)

   a. Proverbs 16:9 _____

   _____

   b. 2 Thessalonians 3:5 _____

   _____

B. The nature of guidance

The chart below outlines ways that God guides people directly and indirectly.

Direct Guidance	Indirect Guidance
1. Spoken revelation from God	1. God's Word
2. Visions	2. Conscience or conviction
3. Dreams	3. Providence (circumstances controlled by God)
4. Prophet/apostle speaking for God	4. Wisdom and counsel

Direct guidance was experienced during the Old Testament and early New Testament time periods. Today, we see God guiding indirectly. The Holy Spirit is active in all areas of indirect guidance as part of His ministry in the believer.

1. Guidance through God's Word

   How does the psalmist describe God's Word (Psalm 119:105)?

   _____

2. Guidance through conviction

   How was Paul stimulated to action in Athens (Acts 17:16)?

   _____

3. Guidance through God's providence

   What can the believer be confident about regardless of the circumstances (Romans 8:28)?

   _____

4. Guidance through God-given wisdom

Read Proverbs 2:1–11. What four things will wisdom allow you to discern (verse 9)?

(1) _____

(2) _____

(3) _____

(4) _____

What is the result of seeking counsel (Proverbs 13:10)? _____

III. Application

A. List one area in which you are wrestling with a decision.

_____

_____

_____

B. Does this issue involve:

☐ God's sovereign will?

☐ God's commanded will?

☐ I don't know which one.

C. What should your response be if it involves:

1. God's sovereign will (Proverbs 3:5–6)?

2. God's commanded will (John 15:10)?

3. You are unsure (James 1:5)?

What action are you going to take?

_____

_____

_____

_____